Black Madonna

Poems

Tayler Simon

Black Madonna

Written by Tayler Simon

First edition

ISBN: 979-8-9986741-2-9

Cover design by Tayler Simon
Interior design by Tayler Simon
Published by Tayler Simon

We shall overcome
WE shall overcome
We SHALL overcome
We shall OVERCOME
WE SHALL OVERCOME

Institution(alized)

I Only Exist in Legislation

I sit here under the watchful sovereign
of John C. Calhoun
the one who fought to
keep my ancestors in bondage

I sit here on
hallowed ground
the house looming above
like the violent father

I am an observant
trying to keep my cards
close to my heart
sitting behind a man in a Trump hat

Proud

These halls are where
I feel most uncomfortable
where my humanity is
debated, legislated, controlled

The banality of legislation
is what makes it dangerous
the freedom of our bodies stripped away
from something as boring
as words on a page

The more of us who show up
the more annoyed they get
because they are reminded
that we are their bosses

The human instinct to survive is strong

Twins

Capitalism and Racism are twins
born from the same father
bred to be their own
types of monsters
still sharing the same DNA

Black Gold

Using Black bodies
to fuel white power
when slavery wasn't enough
when three-fifths wasn't enough
when devouring Black flesh wasn't enough

Authority

I feel trapped in this ivory tower
built on bloodied, Black soil
my value lies in what
I can provide for an institution
erected for me to serve,
for others to benefit
I am relegated to being
the welcome mat

please wipe your feet
before entering
this prestigious institution

Phoenix

My hopelessness says
that these systems are too old
the poison runs too deep

The only thing that will fix this
is the fire burning all
the roots, freeing its hold

Palatable

Not Your Comfort Zone

I am not here
to make you comfortable
my back has been
a footstool for far too long

Palatable

Your speech is so
　　pallid
I mean palatable
I mean so articulate
I mean so white

Where are you from?
not from here
no Southern in your song
all G's in your endings

I learned the code
at a very young age
slipping in and out
as I move between worlds

Not feeling at home
in my Black skin
it's itchy here
it's burning there

I am learning to
love the sound of my voice
but first I need to hear
what I really sound like

Timely

The temerity
to speak up
for dignity

I let it come
bubbling like
a geyser

Spilling forth
though never
quite on time

Spoken Word

We have been taught
to use our inside voice
shrink ourselves to fit
in their neat little boxes

Speaking that word
speaking our truth
project so they can
hear us in the back

More power
More power

The stage is where
we wield that power
channeling our pain
through this pen and mic

I just want to
be heard

How You Sleep At Night

You have the privilege
of laying your head
on your pillow at night
soundly sleeping
with the fact that
my people and I
are focusing on our liberation
and not our revenge

How can you sleep at night?
I guess you lie to yourselves
sing yourself to sleep with your praises
you as hero, us as monsters
with the storybook open to the page
of you standing triumphantly
atop our slain bodies

I hope the angels
remember you with love
and not with vengeance

Black Out

The First Time I Testified

█████████████████████████████████████

████████████████████████████████████ I

am here to speak████████████████████████

As a Black woman████████████████████████

████████████████████████████████████

██████████████████████████████████████

████████ I, █████████████████████████

████████████ was able to ████████████

████████ find community █████████████

████████████████ and create a foundation

of support ██████████████████████████

██████████████████████████████████████

████████████████████████████████████

██████████████████████████████████████

██████████████████████████████████████

██████████████████████████████████████

████████████████ I have seen firsthand ████ the

lack of support for ████████████████████

██████████████████████████████████████

██████████████████████████████████████

██████████████████████████████████████

████████████████ the only Black staff

████████████████ She said

██████████████████████████████████████

nothing could be done. ██████████ didn't
care about me as a person ████████

████████████████████ there were no
resources in place like that ████████

████████ You are ████████

██ stripping away support ████████

School Board January 7, 2025

Thank you for your time here today in listening to the public voice our concerns for our education system. My name is Tayler Simon, and I am a bookstore owner and huge advocate for literacy for all ▓▓▓

The Bluest Eye by Toni Morrison taught me to no longer wish for blue eyes ▓▓▓▓▓▓▓

▓▓▓▓▓▓▓ Alice Walker taught me the quiet power of the connection between Black women. ▓▓▓ Sapphire taught me empathy, for you never know what is going on in someone's ▓▓ life ▓▓▓▓▓

▓▓▓▓▓ Zora Neale Hurston ▓▓▓▓▓▓

▓▓▓ taught me that Black women are not only the mules of the world, but capable of being loved and loving themselves completely.

██ center ██ the stories of women who have historically been seen as less important. ████

████████████████████████████████

████████████████████████████████

████████████████████████████████

████████████████████████████████

████████████████████████████████ wanting to protect children from the harsh realities of the world████████████████████████ to protect that sense of wonder ████ it is irresponsible to coddle ████ It's irresponsible to prioritize the delusion of some ████ at the expense of the whole humanity of other ████ s. ████████

████████████████████████████████

████████████████████████████████

████████████

████████████████████████

████████████████████████████

████████████████ propaganda ████████

████████████ are "indoctrinating" our children ████ values of learning and respecting people and stories that come from all walks of life, ████

████████████████████████████████

████████████████████████████████

████████ is not indoctrination. "Wokeness" has

never driven someone to use violence ███████
and inclusivity is the basis for ████ safety.

██
██
██
████████████████████████████████████ If we
truly care ████████████████████████████ ,
why are we limiting books? ███████████████
██
██
██
██
██ I
believe you all have good in you to do what's right.
██ an Institution is a reflection of our character,
█████████████████ our character reflects
exclusion. █████ reconsider your priorities ████
██ .
██
████████████████████████████████

Instructional Materials Review Committee January 9, 2025

Thank you ▮ for listening ▮▮▮▮▮▮
▮▮▮▮▮▮▮▮▮▮▮▮▮▮▮▮▮▮▮▮
▮▮▮▮▮▮▮▮▮▮▮▮▮▮▮▮▮▮▮▮
▮▮▮▮▮▮▮▮▮▮▮▮▮

If you take a look ▮▮▮▮ on the surface, it is ▮
difficult ▮▮▮▮▮▮ powerful ▮▮▮▮
sheds light on systemic issues like abuse, poverty,
illiteracy, and cycles of trauma. Its raw depiction
▮▮▮▮▮▮▮ seeks to provoke ▮▮▮▮
empathy rather than titillate or exploit. ▮▮
▮▮▮▮▮▮▮▮▮▮▮▮▮▮▮▮▮▮▮▮
▮▮▮▮▮▮▮▮▮▮▮▮▮▮▮▮▮▮▮▮
▮▮▮▮▮▮▮▮▮▮▮▮▮▮▮▮▮▮▮▮
▮▮▮▮▮▮▮▮▮▮▮▮▮▮▮what is
happening in this young person's mind. ▮▮▮
▮▮▮▮▮▮▮▮▮▮▮▮▮▮▮▮▮▮▮▮
▮▮▮▮▮▮▮▮▮▮▮▮▮▮▮▮▮▮▮▮
▮▮▮▮▮▮▮▮▮▮▮▮

Precious was blamed all of her life ▮▮▮▮
▮▮▮▮▮▮▮▮▮▮▮▮▮▮▮▮▮▮▮▮
▮▮▮▮▮▮▮▮▮▮▮▮▮▮▮▮▮▮▮▮

The blame ██████████████ Precious faces█

████████ is mirrored ██████████████ We

reduce███████████████████████████████we

must not see ████████████████████████████

███████████████████████████████████████

█████████████ The█████ details █████ are

█ gratuitous ██████████ to convey the depth

██████████████████████ Sanitizing these

realities diminishes the impact ███████████

███████████████████████████pleasure is

intended ████████████████████████████

███████████████████████████████████████

███████████████████████████████████████

████████████████████. Depictions of abuse are

not intended ███████████

███████████████████████████████████████

█████████ reclaim███ voice and identity. █

███████████████████████████████████████

███████████████████████████████████████

transformation inspires hope and resilience █

███████████████████████████████████████

███████████████████████████████████████

this is a cautionary tale,

for us, the adults,
to see how we fail when we don't

protect them. I ask that you

seek out
community who love

you

29

SC H.3927 March 4, 2025

██████████████████████████████ I am ██ proud ████

██

██

Black, ██

LGBT+, ███

████████████

I ███ came
back to reinvest ██████████████████████ because I
didn't feel welcomed here as a Black woman. █

██

Diversity, Equity, and Inclusion. ████████████████

██

████████ offering views of the world ████████████

████████████████████ familiar or strange. ████████

████████████ mirrors reflecting our own lives and
experiences. ███████████████ this is the very
thread of █████████████████████████████████████

█████████████████████████ the power of storytelling █

████████ more unified communities. ███████████████

██

██

██████████████████████

30

██████████████████████████ become
leaders through the stories ███████████
████████████████ It's ██████ about ████
███████████████████████████████████
███████████████████████████████████
████████████████ giving back to my community.
███████████████████████████████████
███████████████████████████████████
██████████████████████

Diversity, Equity, and Inclusion strengthen our
schools, our businesses, our communities, and our
lives. ███████████████████████████████
███████████████████████████████████
████████████

School Board April 4, 2025

Book bans are not a hoax. ████████████ I care about literacy ████████████ ████ providing more access to books to kids, not less. ██████████████

██████████████ we will be leading the charge ██████████████ ██████████████ for something as heinous as taking books away from children ██████████

████ if you are not concerned ████ ████ you should be ████

████ sexual abuse is not pornographic. ████

you are banning are cautionary tales. ██

32

books touched my life

Shielding our eyes

won't protect them. we are

taking away safe spaces

No one
who removes access to books has ever been on the
right side of history.

33

The Opposite of War Is Creation

Creation Story

There are poems in my bones
and sometimes it hurts
to get them out

If a writer shouts into the void
and no one is there to hear it
did they even say anything?

Here's to feeling
the urge to create
when you feel like
you are being destroyed

Be the Poem

The world needs
to live like a poet
and be the poem

True Self?

When I'm writing
I'm always my truest self
but there's nothing
for me to hide behind
when I put that self
into the world

When They Burn the Books

If I were to write a book
I hope it will be banned
because that would mean
I have something powerful
to say

What I'm Not

I'm not a writer
I'm just a wanderer

I'm not a writer
I'm just a noticer

I'm not a writer
I'm just a dreamer

I'm not a writer
I'm just wishing for love

I'm not a writer
I'm just trapped in my head

Creativity constipation

I want to birth something
to breathe life into something
that isn't serving
someone else's agenda
or dreams
I want to create
something with beauty
and meaning
not for profit

Survival

Alive

Are we doomed
to keep fighting for our lives?
these things feel like cancer
hiding deep in our marrow
changing the coding of our DNA
metastasizing malignancy
over our bodies

One of us has to die

Gratitude Poem

I am thankful for breath
free or caught

I am thankful to be kept
in my grandmother's prayers

I am thankful for this pen
and for my voice

From Poplar Trees

after Strange Fruit by Nina Simone

Violence is more
than what you can do
to my body
to our bodies

No longer Strange Fruit
we are trampled upon the earth
crushed, bruised, rotting
under regulation-issued boots

Bible Study

after Mother Emmanuel

I'm sitting in this tiny room
surrounded by mothers, brothers, aunts, grandfathers
all looking openly with loving curiosity
a thirst for knowledge and liberation

And at any moment during our communion
our doors could open to the world
just like our eyes
just like our arms
and someone with a gun could end it all

Long Game

White supremacy
thinks about seven generations
just like Indigenous practices

We may not win each battle
but we always work to make
our radical imagination a reality

Black Joy

Black Madonna

after Pyramids by Frank Ocean

There is no honor
but to serve
and still be scorned

From temple to club
we are worshipped and revered
but our temples were always defiled

Because what is holy
to those who do not
believe in Her power?

The Gathering Place

There is a cadence
to a black church
a rhythm steeped
in immense loss
a continual overcoming
it is a song
everyone knows
the words to
in the hymnals
of our hearts
it is a movement
swaying as one
a unifying of voices
and in this place
we find all comfort
in the sacrifice

Pour me out
a blessing
so I shall not
have room enough
to receive

Samson (and Delilah)

You are like Samson
drawing strength from your hair

Changing its shape
like the clouds in the sky

Changing its color
like the leaves in autumn

Changing its length, texture, and style
an expression of who you are
and who you want to be

Black. Woman. Joy.

Black women being loved
and unapologetically joyous
and taking up space

Mouths open wide
releasing everything
through their laughter

Head thrown back
eyes closed
you breathe when you laugh
until you can't

To Doechii

Black women create music
with their hair
with their nails
with their praise

Starting with the Mirror

Mirror

If you always
see the world
distorted
how are you to ever
know what is
normal?

Why is it so easy
to believe in other things
but so hard
to believe in yourself?

Me for We

after SNYC speech by W.E.B. DuBois

The Great Sacrifice
calls for struggle
for a time
in order to reach
liberation for a lifetime

You Get to Choose

I want to write
and rest
and be full of joy

I want to love
and cry
and laugh loudly

I want to be free
to be me
not worrying about
other people's
perceptions or expectations

I want to be free
to be me
not worrying

about other
people's perceptions
or expectations

Collage

Who am I when
I'm not saving the world
I am light
I take pieces
Put them together
Stitching something new
From the brokeness

Liberation (or The Natural World)

What Freedom Tastes Like

Is that what freedom tastes like?
can we manufacture
artificial liberation?
bottle it up and sell it
to the masses
like a good capitalist society
can't get high on your own supply
give them enough to get them hooked
and then cut the product
flood it in poor Black neighborhoods
give them something to hope for
and then criminalize them
for wanting more
take what's their birthright
what can't be sold

FM4L

Give me liberation
or give me death
fuck your liberty

The Day the Humans Left

When the humans left
I could breathe a little easier
  the sun shone a little brighter
  the morning air, a little crisper
  the spring rains, a little purer

When the humans left
  I could stretch my limbs higher
  I didn't mind my middle growing rounder
  I love my mane growing fuller
  I can feel my roots growing deeper

I was here before the humans
and I am here now that they've left

If a Tree Falls

Do you know why
a tree is so hard
to cut down?
it's not chopping away
at the bark
the thickness marked by
the passage of time
it's removing the stump
that's left behind
the roots deep
down in the earth

Dreams are easy to see
the growth on the surface
but growth is in the roots
connecting to source
talking to other trees
to let them know when they need
more shade or water or sun

This is how you transform
from a seed

In the Deep Black Soil

I am chasing my dreams
into the dirt
people always look for growth
in the blossoms
the new buds
the big leaves

When you plant a seed
you look for the sprout
a little break through the earth
that tries to find the sun
we don't think about the roots

Bottom Up

Top down never works
we don't start with a tree

     we start with a seed

     we start with the earth

     we start with the rain

     we start with the sun

Together we get the tree
Together we get the forest

Mycelium

I dream of mycelium
of a world where no one
ever has to feel alone

I dream of a world
where people are free
to be themselves
unapologetically
without explanation

I dream of feeling together
where our value is placed
on who we are
as beautiful creatures
and not what we produce

This is a prayer
one I whisper like a mantra

Until I believe it
Until they believe it
Until my ancestors are healed
Until my children are free
Until the land feels whole again

Until we all feel whole again

Acknowledgements

Thank you to my family for always supporting me and my dreams that reach through the soil.

Thank you to my friend Marla, who edited this book and always gasses my writing up.

Thank you to the Modjeska Simkins School through the South Carolina Progressive Network. I wrote many of these poems in those classes.

Thank you to all my comrades whom I can always count on in the work.

Thank you to Jackie, Chio, Karla, Socorro, Jessica, Cam, and Dreya, who gave good feedback for the cover.

Thank you to Bingo and Melanie for starting Shut Up and Write, so I could finish this strong (and Queer Writers of Columbia, The Tree x House, Torch Writing Circle, The Creative Writing Hour, and The Writing Circle)